Another word for home is blackbird

Catherine Wilson Garry

Published in 2023 by Stewed Rhubarb
Tarland, Aberdeenshire
www.stewedrhubarb.org

Editing by Hannah Lavery

Printed & bound by Inky Little Fingers, UK

ISBN: 978-1-910416-26-6

* * *

'Instagram refuses to remove the stolen photos (the
subject is dead)' and 'Collection' were first published in
Interpret Issue 6, April 2022.

'Dulcet' was first published in *Keep Yer Heid* by Coin
Operated Press in 2021.

'In service of a quiet life' was originally written as part of
the BBC Words 1st project in 2021.

'Slice of life' was originally commissioned by the British
National Gallery in 2016.

'Sonder' was first published in the *Speculative Book 2021*
by Speculative Books in 2020.

For my family – those who made me,
those I found, and those we miss.

The exhibit asks 'What is the shape of loss?'

Grief does not have a landscape. It is not
concerned with valleys or birdsong or
even bus stops or a commute to work.

It is, instead, a series of rooms with
carpet that's scuffed where the door
catches it. Where there are forgettable

framed watercolours and box of tissues
on the side table. Where you hand
a woman your wages and still manage

to leave feeling heavier.

Jackdaw

Its wing seems romantic / like a coy eyelash that winks at
the sky / in some form of temptation / like a man loosening
his black tie in a seedy film / the beak suggests an end to an
argument / a sound that ends in a sharpened point / but the
feet are all prehistoric / gnarled, ugly; capable of breaking a
neck / or clutching a thought to carry it away / a crow lands on
the fence / a dinosaur in a magician's cloak reveals its breast.

Birdwatching, part I

When his father died, my dad stopped drinking and
started birdwatching. As if re-shifting his memory

like clearing out an attic. Woodpeckers arrived,
tempted by the Dobbie's premium seed mix,

each one adorned with a red flash atop its head like
a couple of country anarchists.

Just off the bus, I see him
stare through the window

wondering if he is conscious
of the weight he has attached

onto such hollow bones. Until a baby,
fresh to flight, slaps the kitchen window

like a taut wide drum. I've never seen
a man fold like that – as if taking a long letter

to be pushed into an envelope that was never sent –
stuck at the back of a cupboard,

the recipient unable to read it.

October 21st 1995 (the day my father died)

One day, I realised I would never know what he smelled like

unless, he smelled like the box in the attic we kept his clothes in
unless, he smelled like my perfume on his borrowed t-shirts
    my smell, erasing his, like a palimpsest
unless, he smelled like our pet cat who outlived him
    who entered every room surprised, as if still searching

I would never hear his voice
without the distortion of a video camera,
without it being second-hand

I would never get scratched by his beard
      never talk about philosophy
      never play video games
      never call him on a telephone
      never get lost and yell at each other
      never eat something he cooked
      never compare inherited ailments
never watch his hands
as he put a plaster on my knee

And he
      will never meet my friends. Never walk round my flat
      and grumble at the cobwebs.

In a way, he missed out just as much as I did.

Collection

I carry a collection of steps and breaths
in my pocket. The first, my father

on the stairs outside my bedroom.
The second, knowing which drunk flatmate

is turning the key in the lock. The third,
my own, making sure I don't wake

a sleeping house with dressing in the
dark. The last is yours. An exhale

that shows you made it back to me.
The night still hanging on your coat.

Instagram refuses to remove the stolen photos
(the subject is dead)

I check the locks.
I save snowdrop bulbs from an empty wood.

Reclaiming something can feel
the same as protecting it.

I hide my phone. Create hangnails.
I check the locks.

I bury their fat bodies in the garden.
I check the locks.

Fully grown, their heads hang like guilty witnesses.
I eat their hollow bells whole.

At night, white flowers grow from my wrists.
They are so small. So close. So safe.

My grandfather's binoculars

Even though it's been five years
she kept his shoes in the porch

as if he'd step right back into them
and be found, crouching, over something

in the garden. I kept him in my bookcase.
His sons in how they order their lives.

He seemed so lost in life
that it only makes sense for him

to be overwhelmingly present
in death. A beak taps

at the window and I find myself
thinking of his binoculars

how they make the small
so achingly big.

Dulcet

On hearing you read aloud, a fortunate
snark in the audience stated you were stuck

with a mouthful of marbles. As if your tongue was bumping
against the received way to speak. The hand-me-downs

from your mother's West coast lullabies
were diagnosed as impediment.

I wanted to kiss the stones from your mouth,
swallow their dark vowels, until their deep coolness

pooled in my stomach, grounded me
to the wet earth and salt. Instead, I held

your silence. Held the weight of it.

Slice of life

When I was a kid, my mother cut my hair outside,
scattered it for birds' nests
in the hope something could make

a better home out of my split ends.
I feel most at home in other people's.
I like the days that quickly become nights

where we leave conversations feeling
sea-changed, trying to spot the birds
in the park at night. We all exist in

different portions. To some, I might just be cups
left in the sink, a dropped pen, the uncomfortable
warmth on a loo seat. Yet. On the last train home,

my head against a rainy window, I dream
geologists find me. Uncover more than one
wet pavement footprint. Some people only

ever see Van Gogh on a postcard but it
still sits pride of place on a well-worn mantelpiece.

Coming out of lockdown

The world opens like a stocked fridge.
Streets smell like coffee and cigarettes

passed between greedy fingers. Greasy
pizzas, boys showered in Lynx Africa.

I'm a street sommelier, sucking up signs of life
like a fat bee high on abandoned Irn Bru

whilst in the sky, a seagull carries
a jam doughnut in the scissors of his beak.

Olives in St. Giles' Cathedral

Behind the welcome desk
she revealed a bottle from home,

impossibly yellow against the grey
flagstones. I imagined her picking

her way through the shops to find
the ideal weight for him, a colleague

she hardly knew. Her hands testing
the middle spot between embarrassment

and disappointment. I thought
about him; scaring tourists

with his hatred of selfie-sticks.
How we often speak to each other

in such quiet gestures we have to turn our backs
from the magnitudes they contain

like the taste of the oil that flew so many miles
to the kitchen table of his one bedroom flat.

In service of a quiet life

We found a dead frog on the street. Wrapped it
in newspaper and buried it in the bin.

'It's so strange', you said. 'We're so far from
water.' But a lot can be done to cling to normality.

The truth sits on the 6 o'clock news in a nice suit.
Speaks to a man who turns flood into

folklore. An ankle-deep panic,
an empty wave for votes. Those swept away,

are swept under a rug. A hot February is understood
through a joke at a bus stop. Grannies abandon

their cardigans. A lonely politician wins a war.
His wife packs the second-best suitcase.

We cross the road without looking and get hit by a car. So,
what happens here, then? A crisp packet sits

on the same hill for centuries. A feminist sweat shop t-shirt
puts flies into the same spider's web. In the forest,

I put my ear to the bell of a daffodil. I swear
it rings like an alarm. Cows sit down

before it rains. Do they know what's coming?
In the night I imagine our bed has changed;

become new. Become lifeboat.

Sonder

Every time we walk down the street
a thousand lives buzz

around our heads like honey bees
busily homing their lives.

I share my streets with

    philosophers,
    builders,
    lawyers,
    runners,
    trombone players,
    tram conductors,
    women
        who wanted to be scientists when they grew up,
    the picture book writer who stamps
        inspiration into the pillow creases of small minds.

I want to snap this crown in half to gift it
    to the sad faces pressed on the bus windows,
    or the young widows, or the elderly
    who still volunteer every Sunday,

    or the little girl who gets bullied at school
    for the way her front tooth refuses to fit in.

I want to love these clumsy gods
until my heart breaks. Until I can't

conjure up the words to do humanity justice.
Until the only skill I can write on my CV

to explain the gaps is:
'people watching, 22 years.'

I am lucky enough to be watching
the first stone dropped in the pond

and see its ripple buzzing
forever around my architecture.

In the late-night small-talk of memento mori,
of the first poem on that stage that stays

long after the microphone is switched off.
In the quiet nights in, where love is soldered

and burns so bright the lightbulbs
shatter off at what they have witnessed.

I want to collect more stones
pebble-dash my pockets until

I am heavy with possibility.
Leave them instead of flowers

that float away on the breeze –
their presence persistently marking

once: they were here, they did this,
watch the sand shift around their existence.

From
>
> the bus driver who builds the schedules
> to the barista who brews the start of the day
>
> like an orchestral warm-up
>
> to the students with two eyes on tomorrow
> to the protestors with two fists at the past
>
> to the musicians who spend no time practicing
> because they're too busy tuning songs into pitches
>
> to the librarian who categorises creation
> to the nurses and postmen,
>
> the teachers and rail workers,
> the cleaners and call-centre agents –

I want the world to hold you better.
For your joy to be unshakeable,

for the streets to float with the
faces you hit with your everyday miracles.

In the winter, a bumblebee queen shakes
her whole body to keep her eggs warm.

The movement of one is felt for a lifetime.

Pigeon

Your nests are shite, mate
no attempt at architecture
which roll away

and then I remember

and somehow
and missing feet
that demand we ignore

somehow
you're here

in the gap of every city
like the wildflowers

fodder for mockery
or consideration for your unborn,
like dropped pennies

the breeding
the post rooms
the science labs

against the odds of pet cats
and angry signs at train stations
you
and starve you

and the soundtrack of every walk
that grow through the concrete.

Going over to the ghost side

After Tove Jansson

Our love is a secret love. An envelope
sealed shut with a lick. I have hidden

it in the attic. Amongst the fishing tackle,
the cartoon offcuts, ramshackle trolls.

We meet there, in the middle, to share
our talk of a summer house. Where we can

let the saltwater mingle with our blood. And later,
we wake simultaneously in separate beds.

Hush

Like the silence before an orchestra, two crisp packets
dance between the lampposts. Coupled

pigeons bed down in their first home. A pair
of wet shoes hang on the fence, linking

their laces together like a promise.
Behind the glass, a widower

greets the morning with a cup of tea.

Birdwatching, part II

When it is too much
I take myself birdwatching.

This practice is not about collection;
or identification; or, even, knowledge.

It is about movement. It is about the
thrum beneath a tiny chest. It is about

the dead beetles in the dirt. The dried
up patches of dirt. It is about the

humble species like blackbirds and
house sparrows and wrens and

(when it is too much) perhaps even seagulls.
It is about the way our lives are so small

so painfully small. It is their ignorance held
like a handful of walnuts. I borrow it for now.

Magpie

I love the gorgeous cheek of you. The refusal
to fit to human concepts of property and
ownership. I have counted you like prayer

beads. Held your name in my mouth
like a good luck charm. Saluted you
from pedestrian crossings and exam

hall windows. And I know, when I
wonder if I have seen the same bird
twice, the feeling will never be

mutual. But when you skirt the rain
to sit next to my window, I hope you
know, your magic still sits with me.

Blackbird

Before he was my husband, he told
me that another word for home
was blackbird. What else feels as

reliable as that call, the opening of the
year, which all other birds
can only hope to catch up to?

When I am travel-drunk in airports, the
first noise I hear is them –
yelling at a lamppost.

We look out the window,
of the house he grew
up in, and I am thankful

for the blackbirds we have
found together.

Acknowledgements

Some thank yous are due for the creation of this pamphlet.

First of all, to Duncan Lockerbie and Charlie Roy at Stewed Rhubarb Press for seeing the potential in these poems and giving them such a supportive home. Thank you too to Hannah Lavery for editing these poems – this collection is so much better for your insight.

So much of my writing as a whole has come from the spoken word nights across Edinburgh and Glasgow which provided space for me to listen, learn, share and improve my work – as well as build life-long friendships. I am so thankful to: the Soapbox open mic, the Edinburgh University Literature Society poetry slams, Inky Fingers, Aloud QMU, Sonnet Youth, Rock the Boat as well as StAnza Poetry Festival in St. Andrew's. There are doubtless more, and Scottish spoken word, and all the hard workers and writers on and off stage continues to inspire me.

Specific thanks are due to those who gave me time and feedback (and friendship!) including the Poets Exchange group, the University of Edinburgh slam team and our captain Toby Campion, Heather Parry and, more generally, the audiences and poets I have shared spaces with who have shared insight and advice, or just helped foster a space to grow.

Thank you too to BBC Words First and Scottish Youth Theatre for giving me space and time to improve my work. I am also incredibly grateful for Writing West Midlands' workshops hosted by Liz Berry, which gave me so much inspiration and a better understanding of my writing.

For my parents, who aren't sure if poetry is a proper job, but are always more than ready to support it.

To Douglas, for everything.

Stewed Rhubarb is Charlie Roy and Duncan Lockerbie. We are a small, inclusive and independent Scottish press that champions new and diverse poetry.

www.stewedrhubarb.org

STEWED RHUBARB